THE JEHOVAH'S WITNESSES' BIBLE

An Evaluation of the Text of the New World Translation

GIUSEPPE GUARINO

Sixth Edition: October, 2023

Author: Giuseppe Guarino

Layout and Cover: Giuseppe Guarino

e-mail: guarinous@yahoo.com

www.giuseppeguarino.com

To my Jehovah's Witnesses friends

CONTENTS

Introduction 9

PART ONE - THE TRANSLATION OF PASSAGES REVEALING THAT JESUS IS GOD

Introducing the Problem 13
John 1:1 15
John 8:58 25
Acts 20:28 31
Romans 9:5 35
Colossians 1:15-18 39
Colossians 2:9 43
Philippians 2:5-7 47
Philippians 2:9 51
Titus 2:13 – 2 Peter 1:1 55
Hebrews 1:7-12 61

PART TWO - TEXTUAL PROBLEMS

Introduction 69
John 1:18 73
John 3:13 77
1 Timothy 3:16 81
1 John 5:7-8 85

PART THREE - THE DEITY OF JESUS IN THE NEW WORLD TRANSLATION

Introduction 91

John 20:26-28 93
1 John 5:20 95

PART FOUR - THE NAME OF GOD AND THE NEW TESTAMENT

Introduction 101
Manuscript Evidence 105
Internal Evidence 107
The Tetragram and the LXX 113
Conclusions 117

PART FIVE – CONCLUSION

Conclusion 121

Appendix A - Journal Of Biblical Literature:
P. Harner: Qualitative Anarthrous Predicate Nouns 123

Bibliography 131

About the Author 133

INTRODUCTION

The New World Translation (NWT) is the official translation of the Bible released by the Watch Tower, the Jehovah's Witnesses' Directive Body. The first English edition was presented to the public in 1950. The latest updated edition is the 2013's, now available online.

It is a very peculiar version of the Bible.

In this book I will direct the readers' attention to the evident mistakes that make of the NWT a unique literary phenomenon among the various attempts of translating the Bible. These mistakes are so many and so misleading on certain specific doctrines that I cannot help but wonder if we are looking instead of a translation at a deliberate attempt to manipulate the text of the Scripture. This the readers will judge by themselves.

In the first part of the book I will focus my attention on the New Testament passages where the Deity of Jesus has been removed or made obscure, considering as simply as I can the grammar of the original Greek text of the New Testament.

In the second and fourth part I will discuss the critical text adopted by the NWT and its choice to include the name of God, *Jehovah,* in the New Testament.

The third part will be a quick look at passages in the NWT which still bear witness to the deity of Jesus.

My goal is to make this work a quick reference book and a tool in the hands of the believer whenever Jehovah's Witnesses will knock on their doors so that he or she will be able to answer to their false pretenses on the New World Translation reliability.

The info I collected and used here comes from the very good official website that the Watch Tower has built, www.jw.org, which is absolutely very useful for quick access to information that in the past was very hard to collect.

May God help us not to be arguers only, but good witnesses of His grace.

PART ONE

The mis-translation of passages revealing that Jesus is God

INTRODUCING THE PROBLEM

In this first section I will discuss of those Bible passages which clearly teach that Jesus is God in the original Greek but that the Watch Tower has not translated accurately, altering the simple truth they reveal, in order to better substantiate their unscriptural position on the person of Jesus.

I will evaluate these passages in the light of my experience on the original text of the New Testament, quoting, when necessary, from grammars and manuals.

The critical text that I will use as a reference is the *The Greek New Testament According to the Majority Text* edited by Zane C. Hodges and Arthur L. Farstad, Thomas Nelson Publishers, Nashville. Anyway, most of the passages I quote in this study are the same with the prestigious Nestle-Aland text, which the JW seem to be so fond of.

For the English text I will use the New King James Version as a constant reference, but honestly, concerning the Deity of Jesus, I might use any other Bible translation, both old and new.

One important detail is that, up until now, the Watch Tower has not released an official grammar for the New Testament Greek. This is why, absurd as it may seem, they quote from grammars and texts that ultimately contradict or do not share their views.

It is incredible how they extensively quote Harner in a passage where, if read all, he affirms the divinity of the Son of God. Just like they quote Howard to motivate their inclusion of Jehovah in the New Testament – notwithstanding the fact that he has openly asked the Watch Tower to stop misusing his studies.

JOHN 1:1

The original Greek Text
'Εν ἀρχῇ ἦν ὁ Λόγος, καὶ ὁ Λόγος ἦν πρὸς τὸν Θεόν, καὶ Θεὸς ἦν ὁ Λόγος.

Commonly accepted English Translation
In the beginning was the Word, and the Word was with God, and the Word was God.

New World Translation 2013
In the beginning was the Word, and the Word was with God, and the Word was a god.

In the footnotes they give an alternative to "a god", which is "divine"

Both "a god" and "divine" are wrong. God is the right translation of the last sentence of verse 1.

Let us explain why to the reader.

Grammar

I like the text of "The Amplified Bible", which gives the reader a better idea of the meanings involved in the Greek original of this passage.

It reads: "In the beginning [before all time] was the Word ([a]Christ), and the Word was with God, and [b]the Word was God Himself."

The Greek makes it plain that the Word was eternal, that it was with God, was a separate being from the Father, but that, at the same time, like Him, He is God.

Let the NWT explain the reasons why they choose to translate "a god."

"Does John 1:1 prove that Jesus is God?

John 1:1, *RS:* "In the beginning was the Word, and the Word was with God, and the Word was God [also *KJ, JB, Dy, Kx, NAB*]." *NE* reads "what God was, the Word was." *Mo* says "the Logos was divine." *AT* and *Sd* tell us "the Word was divine." The interlinear rendering of *ED* is "a god was the Word." *NW* reads "the Word was a god"; *NTIV* uses the same wording.

What is it that these translators are seeing in the Greek text that moves some of them to refrain from saying "the Word was God"? The definite article (the) appears before the first occurrence of *the·os'* (God) but not before the second. The articular (when the article appears) construction of the noun points to an identity, a personality, whereas a singular anarthrous (without the article) predicate noun before the verb (as the sentence is constructed in Greek) points to a quality about someone. So the text is not saying that the Word (Jesus) was the same as the God *with whom* he was but, rather, that the Word was godlike, divine, a god."[1]

If I can be entirely honest, such statements made by the JW leaders seem to echo words which were spoken a long time ago, and that caused the beginning of humanity's troubles: "*...Yea, hath God said, Ye shall not eat of every tree of the garden*?" (Genesis 3:1)

Why am I saying this?

Because what the WT wrote is basically true. In fact, the Bible says that Jesus is not the same with the Father, they are, we say for lack of a better human term, two persons. The conjunction "with" (πρὸς) of John 1:1 clearly implies that. But, though not the same individual, the two are both God.

On jw.org we read that: "The articular (when the article appears) construction of the noun points to an identity, a personality, whereas a singular anarthrous (without the article) predicate noun before the verb (as the sentence is constructed in Greek) points to a quality about someone."

They are right.

Just like when Satan quoted the Scriptures to Jesus: "*And saith unto him, If thou be the Son of God, cast thyself down: for it is written, He shall give his angels charge concerning thee: and in their hands they shall bear thee up, lest at any time thou dash thy foot against a stone.*" (Matthew 4:6 - KJV)

That is why we need to add to what the WT writes, just like Jesus did with the partial truth spoken by the Devil, the fact that if "theos" is qualitative, it cannot be indefinite, it cannot be translated "a god."

---

[1]Source:https://wol.jw.org/en/wol/d/r1/lp-e/1101989240 (05/08/2019)

"When a substantive is anarthrous, it may have one of the three forces: indefinite, qualitative or definite." Daniel B. Wallace, *Greek Grammar Beyond the Basics*, p. 243.

So, first JW convince us that "*theos*" is qualitative, then they translate it as indefinite!

I wonder if they realize what they are saying. Their attitude is of someone who has to prove his preconceived ideas.

When I learned Greek I did not do it to prove my point on anything I believed, but to better understand the Scriptures. I did not simply learn through the grammars, but, like I did with English, through extensive practice and reading. I am not paid by any religious organization, I serve God and the Truth, to bless the body of Christ. If I had found in the Scriptures that Jesus was not God I would have had no problem to say that. But, on the contrary, reading the New Testament in the original has convinced me even the more that our Lord was truly God made man.

How many JW would dare openly state their doubts about the WT's teachings? It is not easy to face the results of expressing an idea contrary to the organization when you are a part of it – and still hope to enjoy the benefits of being a part of it.

Anyway, the Watch Tower makes other quotations on this passage which are certainly worth being cited here.

"In his article "Qualitative Anarthrous Predicate Nouns: Mark 15:39 and John 1:1," published in *Journal of Biblical Literature,* Vol. 92, Philadelphia, 1973, p. 85, Philip B. Harner said that such clauses as the one in John 1:1, "with an anarthrous predicate preceding the verb, are primarily qualitative in meaning. They indicate that the *logos* has the nature of *theos*. There is no basis for regarding the predicate *theos* as definite." On p. 87 of his article, Harner concluded: "In John 1:1 I think that the qualitative force of the predicate is so prominent that the noun cannot be regarded as definite."[2]

Again, they quote against their choice to translate the predicate as indefinite, because it is qualitative! They should make up their mind: is it qualitative or indefinite?

I subscribe to their quotations, in fact it is just because it is qualitative that the correct translation is: "and the Word was God."

Jesus has the quality of God, but he is distinct from the Father.

Let us consider one simple example to understand how a qualitative predicate must be dealt with.

In 1 John 1:5 the Greek reads " *ὁ θεὸς φῶς ἐστὶν*" (ho Theos phos estin). The word "*φῶς*", "light" has no article, it is obviously qualitative. This is why the NWT correctly translates this verse: "*God is light*" and not "God is a light", because qualitative does not mean indefinite! It is not correct to translate a qualitative predicate using the English indefinite article. This is why, being "*Theos*" of John 1:1 is qualitative (and not indefinite) as the Watch Tower itself took the pain to extensively prove, and by consequence it does not require the indefinite article in the translation.

It is indeed ridiculous that the WT continues to quote from Harner. In fact, he explains perfectly what he actually meant to say in the sentence **mis-quoted** by JW: "But in all of these cases the English reader might not understand exactly what John was trying to express.

---

[2] Source: https://wol.jw.org/en/wol/d/r1/lp-e/1001060096 (05/08/2019)

Perhaps the clause could be translated, "the Word had the same nature as God." This would be one way of representing John's thought, which is, as I understand it, that **ho logos**, no less than **ho theos**, had the nature of **theos**."

If you do not believe what I say here, read the article yourself. Philip B. Harner, "Qualitative Anarthrous Predicate Nouns, Mark 15:39 and John 1:1" (**Journal of Biblical Literature**, March 1973), 92:75-87.

Those who quoted did not read it all? If they did, didn't they truly realize what they were doing in partially quoting? Or are they just like the Devil, partially quoting Scriptures to cast doubt and confusion?

At the end of this book, in an Appendix, I will reproduce the entire text of Harner's article.

A Manual Grammar of the New Testament by H.E. Dana e Julius R. Mantey, one of my favorite Greek grammars, explains why the article is missing in John 1:1.

"πρὸς τὸν Θεόν (with God) points to Christ's fellowship with the person of the Father; Θεὸς ἦν ὁ Λόγος (the Word is God) emphasizes Christ's participation in the essence of the divine nature. The former clearly applies to personality, while the latter applies to character." (p. 140)

John avoided a language that could lead the reader to understand that Jesus is God the Father. Had he written "ὁ Θεὸς ἦν ὁ Λόγος", that's what we could have understood. On the contrary, the beloved apostle was very careful in telling us in a clear language that Jesus is God, but not the Father.

Context

John 1:1 must be considered in its context – like any other text that we hope to understand correctly. Reading the first eighteen verses of John, let us notice how he deals with Greek predicates and nouns.

The word "Theos" is found 8 times in the first 18 verses of John. The article is present in three occurrences, in verse 1 and 2. The rest of the times it has no article!

This is how the NWT translates the other anarthrous occurrences of "*Theos*" in those passages:

V. 6, "*There came a man who was sent as a representative of God;*"

V. 12 "*However, to all who did receive him, he gave authority to become God's children,*"

V. 13 "*And they were born, not from blood or from a fleshly will or from man's will, but from God.*"

V. 18 "*No man has seen God at any time;*"

It is not necessary to be a philologist to understand that it is impossible according to logic, style, consistency and even common sense, to believe that in only 18 verses John can use the word "*Theos*" six times, but in only one instance he wants the reader to understand a different meaning than that plainly intended in the other five times he uses the same term.

Let us consider some similar occurrences in these same verses, to further investigate the writing style of the apostle John.

The word "Only begotten", is present both with and without the article (*ho monoghenes – monoghenes*) in verses 14 and 18.

The word "father" is with the article in verse 18 and without in verse 14.

The word "man" has the article in verse 4 and doesn't have in verses 6 and 9.

In the same verse 4 the word "life" occurs twice, with and without the article.

In verse 14 also the word "glory" occurs twice, with and without the article.

The word "grace" does not have the article in verse 14 but has it in verse 17, which is the same thing that happens with the word "truth."

In all these cited instances, words have the same meaning whether they have or don't have the article preceding them.

In the light of this, it is impossible – not improbable, but absolutely impossible – that by omitting an article John has used a word to express a total different meaning in one specific passage only.

The Original Text

Εἶπεν αὐτοῖς ὁ Ἰησοῦς· Ἀμὴν ἀμὴν λέγω ὑμῖν, πρὶν Ἀβραὰμ γενέσθαι ἐγώ εἰμι.

The NKJV

Jesus said to them, 'Most assuredly, I say to you, before Abraham was, I AM.'

The New World Translation

Jesus said to them: 'Most truly I say to you, before Abraham came into existence, I have been.'

The NWT does not accept the literal translation, the embarrassing "I AM" used by Jesus. But, instead of throwing stones to silence the Lord, like the Jews did, they (ab)use the Greek and English grammar to do so.

The "I am" uttered here by Jesus follows the many other instances found in the fourth Gospel.

The WT explains why the "I am" can and must be translated here in English as "I have been" to be consistent with the English language.

"The action expressed in John 8:58 started "before Abraham came into existence" and is still in progress. In such situation εἰμι, which is the first - person singular present indicative, is properly translated by the perfect indicative." So far their opinion.

Ok.

I don't think they are right anyway. But, let's just say they are right. What does this change in the original Greek? You may translate it as you wish, yet the Greek remains "I am". This is incontrovertible. Am I being too obvious?

Truth is JW have a tendency to drag their listeners inside their fighting pit of endless, useless arguments.

Let us ask a very important question: What would the Greek speaking reader – who knew nothing then of the English language – understand when confronted with this passage?

First of all, he will be prepared to read of a deep truth, since the phrase uttered by Jesus is introduced by the peculiar expression of the gospel of John, "Αμὴν ἀμὴν", which is literally: "Amen, Amen." John uses here the Hebrew transliterated into Greek. It's done by the other evangelists too, but the repetition of the term twice is found only in John.

After this we notice the two verbs present here: the "γενέσθαι" used for the "being" of Abraham, his "coming into existence", is in open contrast with the verb "εἰμι" referred to Jesus.

The Greek speaking reader of this passage would recall the words used in this same gospel, at its opening.

Ἐν ἀρχῇ **ἦν** (past tense verb εἰμι) ὁ λόγος,
In the beginning was the Word

καὶ ὁ λόγος **ἦν** πρὸς τὸν θεόν,
and the Word was with God

καὶ θεὸς **ἦν** ὁ λόγος.
And the Word was God.

Οὗτος **ἦν** ἐν ἀρχῇ πρὸς τὸν θεόν.
He was in the beginning with God

The Word was in the beginning. The verb used is "to be", "εἰμι", which in Greek speaks of absolute existence. The verb used for created things, things that come into being *ex-nihilo*, is another one, the same used in John 8:58 for the birth of Abraham, "γίνομαι." In fact after the verb used for the Word, the past tense conjugation of "εἰμι", John introduces the creation of the world using the conjugations of "γίνομαι."

Πάντα δι' αὐτοῦ **ἐγένετο**,
All through him came into being

καὶ χωρὶς αὐτοῦ
and without him

ἐγένετο οὐδὲ ἓν ὃ **γέγονεν**.
Came into being nothing of that which came into being.

Ἐν αὐτῷ ζωὴ ἦν.
In him was Life.

In the Word was life, it never was given Him: he has always been and is the cause of all creation with the Father.

Going back to John 8:58, this is what the Greek tells us, this is what Jesus actually said: Abraham was born, but I never had a beginning.

This fact cannot be changed by a mis-translation of the Greek text, simply because a translation cannot determine the meaning of an original.

Before pronouncing this very powerful "I am" the Lord said something very important.

"Your father Abraham rejoiced to see My day, and he saw it and was glad."

Then the Jews said to Him, "You are not yet fifty years old, and have You seen Abraham?"

Jesus said to them, "Most assuredly, I say to you, before Abraham was, I AM."

What was Jesus speaking about when he said that Abraham saw his day? And, are the words spoken at the climax of his speech to be related to those spoken to Moses in Exodus 3?

The endless arguing of the JWs over this passage cannot let us lose focus on the importance of Jesus' statements here: Jesus was referring to himself as appearing to the patriarch Abraham when, before his incarnation, he was the Word John chapter one speaks about…

Honestly, it would be too long to discuss here the deep theological implications of these verses. I will leave the intelligent reader with the words of Justin Martyr, a Christian who lived in the second century and wrote concerning this matter. He writes: "Permit me, further, to show you from the book of Exodus how this same One, who is both Angel and God, and Lord, and man, and who appeared in human form to Abraham and Isaac, appeared in a flame of fire from the bush, and conversed with Moses." Justin Martyr, *Dialogue with Trypho*, Chapter LIX, Ante-Nicene Fathers, Volume 1, Hendrickson Publishers, Peabody, Massachusetts, USA, 1994, p. 226.

Justin's mother tongue was Greek! I strongly urge the honest seeker of the Truth to read his writing, very easy to find online, since it is of public domain.

John 8:58 speaks of Jesus as the eternal Son of the Living God. Any mis-translation or even good translation cannot change what the context and the original language clearly state.

The Original Text

προσέχετε οὖν ἑαυτοῖς καὶ παντὶ τῷ ποιμνίῳ, ἐν ᾧ ὑμᾶς τὸ Πνεῦμα τὸ Ἅγιον ἔθετο ἐπισκόπους, ποιμαίνειν τὴν ἐκκλησίαν τοῦ Θεοῦ, ἣν περιποιήσατο διὰ τοῦ ἰδίου αἵματος.

The NKJV

Therefore take heed to yourselves and to all the flock, among which the Holy Spirit has made you overseers, to shepherd the church of God which He purchased with His own blood.

The NWT

Pay attention to yourselves and to all the flock, among which the holy spirit has appointed you overseers, to shepherd the congregation of God, which he purchased with the blood of his own Son.

The simple comment to make here is that the word "Son" is simply not in the original text.

In the previous versions of the NWT words added to the text were put between brackets. So at least the readers knew that some words had been added that were not in the Greek – legitimately or illegitimately the reader could have judged by himself.

In the most recent version of the NWT there are no brackets to reveal these additions to their Bible readers, who have all reasons, trusting the Watch Tower, to believe that what they are reading is part of the original text.

To conclude that the blood spoken about here is that of His Son is not the task of a translator, but of an interpreter – two separate roles, two different ways of approaching the text.

Removal of brackets for the words added to the original text (which were present in previous versions) is a sad characteristic of the latest edition of the NWT, the one available now online. (05/13/2019)

The Original Greek Text
ὧν οἱ πατέρες, καὶ ἐξ ὧν ὁ Χριστὸς τὸ κατὰ σάρκα, ὁ ὢν ἐπὶ πάντων Θεὸς εὐλογητὸς εἰς τοὺς αἰῶνας· ʽΑμήν.

The NKJV
… of whom are the fathers and from whom, according to the flesh, Christ came, who is over all, the eternally blessed God. Amen.

The NWT
To them the forefathers belong, and from them the Christ descended according to the flesh. God, who is over all, be praised forever. Amen.

The translation stating the deity of Jesus seems to be the most natural conclusion of a Christological hymn, but since punctuation was not in the original text of the New Testament, we must admit that both versions are possible.

Hippolytus is a Christian who lived between the end of the second century and the beginning of the third. He is listed among the so called Greek Fathers of the Church. He writes: "Let us look next at the apostle's word: "Whose are the fathers, of whom as concerning the flesh Christ came, who is over all, God blessed forever." This word declares the mystery of the truth rightly and clearly. He is over all is God; for thus He speaks boldly, "All things are delivered unto me of my Father." He who is over all, God blessed, has been born; and having been made man, He is (yet) God for ever. For to this effect John also has said, "who is, and who was, and who is to come, the Almighty." And well has he named Christ the Almighty." Hippolytus, *Against the Heresy of One Noetus,* Ante-Nicene Fathers, Volume 5, Hendrickson Publishers, Peabody, Massachusetts, USA, 1994, p. 225.

The Original Text

ὅς ἐστιν εἰκὼν τοῦ Θεοῦ τοῦ ἀοράτου, πρωτότοκος πάσης κτίσεως, ὅτι ἐν αὐτῷ ἐκτίσθη **τὰ πάντα**, τὰ ἐν τοῖς οὐρανοῖς καὶ τὰ ἐπὶ τῆς γῆς, τὰ ὁρατὰ καὶ τὰ ἀόρατα, εἴτε θρόνοι, εἴτε κυριότητες εἴτε ἀρχαὶ εἴτε ἐξουσίαι· **τὰ πάντα** δι' αὐτοῦ καὶ εἰς αὐτὸν ἔκτισται· καὶ αὐτός ἐστι **πρὸ πάντων** καὶ **τὰ πάντα** ἐν αὐτῷ συνέστηκε, καὶ αὐτός ἐστιν ἡ κεφαλὴ τοῦ σώματος, τῆς ἐκκλησίας· ὅς ἐστιν ἀρχή, πρωτότοκος ἐκ τῶν νεκρῶν, ἵνα γένηται ἐν πᾶσιν αὐτὸς πρωτεύων.

The NKJV

15 He is the image of the invisible God, the firstborn
over all creation. 16 For by Him all things were created
that are in heaven and that are on earth, visible and
invisible, whether thrones or dominions or principalities
or powers. All things were created through Him and for
Him. 17 And He is before all things, and in Him all things
consist. 18 And He is the head of the body, the church,
who is the beginning, the firstborn from the dead, that in
all things He may have the preeminence.

The NWT

15 He is the image of the invisible God, the firstborn
of all creation; 16 because by means of him **all other**

things were created in the heavens and on the earth, the things visible and the things invisible, whether they are thrones or lordships or governments or authorities. **All other things** have been created through him and for him. [17] Also, he is before **all other things**, and by means of him **all other things** were made to exist, [18] and he is the head of the body, the congregation. He is the beginning, the firstborn from the dead, so that he might become the one who is first in all things;

For four times the NWT translates "all **other** things" where the original text has "all things."

This is not translating, this is adulterating the meaning of a text by adding words which are not part of the original Greek.

The Kingdom Interlinear Translation of the Greek Scriptures reveals it clearly that this word is not even in the Greek original adopted by the NWT.

The intent is clear, by adding this little word "other", the WT implies that Jesus was among the created beings. On the contrary, the literal translations exclude the possibility of Jesus being created "For by Him **all things** were created."

The Greek here is "τὰ πάντα" which means "all things." The word "other" is simply not there. You need only some basic knowledge of the Greek language to know this.

The expression "τὰ πάντα" occurs about 36 times in the New Testament.

It is found also in Colossians 3:11, where the NWT has: "*where there is neither Greek nor Jew, circumcision nor uncircumcision, foreigner, Scyth'i·an, slave, or freeman; but Christ is all things* (Greek: τὰ πάντα) *and in all.*"

Let's read the NWT in 1 Corinthians 15:28: "*But when all things* (τὰ πάντα) *will have been subjected to him, then the Son himself will also subject himself to the One who subjected all things* (τὰ πάντα) *to him, that God may be all things* (πάντα) *to everyone.*"

Here in Colossians we are looking at a deliberate manipulation of the text in order to adapt it to the thoughts and beliefs of the Watch Tower by removing the reference to the eternity of the Son of God.

In the previous versions of the NWT, here like in other passages, square brackets told the readers words had been added to the original text – for whatever purpose. Today's NWT updated edition is not so kind with its readers.

COLOSSIANS 2:9

The Original Text
ὅτι ἐν αὐτῷ κατοικεῖ πᾶν τὸ Πλήρωμα τῆς θεότητος σωματικῶς.

The NKJV
For in Him dwells all the fullness of the Godhead bodily.

The NWT
Because it is in him that all the fullness of the divine quality dwells bodily.

In Colossian 2:9 we have a wonderful Greek word, θεότητος (theotetos). This word speaks of essence, which must be distinguished from quality. Of course the NWT either ignores this fact or is totally lack of any interest for it and translates "divine quality" what must evidently be seen as a reference to and must be translated as "Godhead."

"In the Latin versions, owing to the poverty of the language, both *θεότης* (theotes) and *θειότης* (theiotes) are translated by the same term *divinitas*; but this was felt to be inadequate, and the word *deitas* was coined at a later date to represent θεότης." J. B. Lightfoot, D.D., D.C.L., L.L.D., *St. Paul's Epistles to the Colossians and Philemon*, Hendrickson Publishers, Third Printing, August 1995, p.182

The NWT tries to remove the significance of Paul's sentence by avoiding such powerful and meaningful terminology. In doing so, the beautiful *crescendo* of the original words of Paul miserably collapses in the poor translation "divine quality."

In Romans 1:20, Paul used the word "θειότης", and it clearly indicates the divine quality. He knew that word, but here he chose another. But, even in Romans the sentence cannot be understood of a secondary state of divinity, but as a quality of the supreme God: "For his invisible qualities are clearly seen from the world's creation onward, because they are perceived by the things made, even his eternal power and Godship, so that they are inexcusable." (NWT)

The NWT is wrong in Colossians 2:9, or, at least inaccurate. It is another poor attempt to obliterate a clear reference to the Deity of the Son of God.

In any respect, even if wrong, the WT's version only moves the attention from essence to quality, which is nowhère stated to be understood as a lesser divine quality – on the contrary, the context openly speaks of the glory of the Son.

The power of terminology in Colossians 2:9 is incredible.

"It is evident, I think, from the passages in St Paul, that the word πλήρωμα, 'fulness, plenitude', must have had a more or less definite theological value when he wrote. This inference, which is suggested by the frequency of the word, seems almost inevitable when we consider the form of the expression in the first passage quoted, Col. 1.19. The absolute use of the word, πᾶν τὸ πλήρωμα, 'all the fulness', would otherwise be unintelligible, for it does not explain itself. [...] The sense in which St Paul employs this term was doubtless the sense which he found already attached to it. He means, as he explicitly states in the second Christological passage of the Colossian Epistle (2:9), the pleroma, the plenitude of 'the Godhead' or 'of Deity'. In the first passage (1:9), though the word stands without the addition *τῆς θεότητος*, the signification required by the context is the same." J. B. Lightfoot, D.D., D.C.L., L.L.D., *St. Paul's Epistles to the Colossians and Philemon*, Hendrickson Publishers, Third Printing, August 1995, p. 261, 262.

The Original Text

Τοῦτο γὰρ φρονείσθω ἐν ὑμῖν ὃ καὶ ἐν Χριστῷ Ἰησοῦ, ὃς ἐν μορφῇ Θεοῦ ὑπάρχων, οὐχ ἁρπαγμὸν ἡγήσατο τὸ εἶναι ἴσα Θεῷ, ἀλλ᾽ ἑαυτὸν ἐκένωσε μορφὴν δούλου λαβών, ἐν ὁμοιώματι ἀνθρώπων γενόμενος.

The NKJV

5 Let this mind be in you which was also in Christ
Jesus, 6 who, being in the form of God, did not consider
it robbery to be equal with God, 7 but made Himself of
no reputation, taking the form of a bondservant, *and*
coming in the likeness of men.

The NWT

Keep this mental attitude in you that was also in Christ Jesus, who, although he was existing in God's form, gave no consideration to a seizure, namely, that he should be equal to God. No, but he emptied himself and took a slave's form and became human.

This passage is not easy to translate. But what the NWT does to it is absolutely not translating, simply because the phrase: "gave no consideration to a seizure, namely, that he should be equal to God" does not translate the Greek, but forces it into the preconceived ideas of the Watch Tower.

The text openly says that Jesus was in "μορφῇ Θεοῦ", "form of God", was God already. All the words the NWT adds to the Greek text pervert its meaning in order to let it say that Jesus did not attempt to become equal to God. But the text already said He was God!

The wonderful truth revealed here is simple and glorious. Jesus,

ἐν μορφῇ Θεοῦ ὑπάρχων
in the form of God being

μορφὴν δούλου λαβών
form of servant taking

The passage speaks of Jesus who being God, was anyway ready to abandon his state, leave His glory in Heaven to become a man for us. This passage speaks of the endless love of Jesus for us.

This another possible version: "Though He pre-existed in the form of God, yet he did not look upon equality with God as a prize which must not slip from His grasp, but He empties Himself, divested Himself, taking upon Him the form of a slave." This is J. B. Lightfoot expanded translation.

I like the Amplified Bible, which renders the idea of the original text very well: "Let this same attitude and purpose and [humble] mind be in you which was in

Christ Jesus: [Let Him be your example in humility] Who, although being essentially one with God and in the form of God [possessing the fullness of the attributes which make God God], did not [think this equality with God was a thing to be eagerly grasped or retained, But stripped Himself [of all privileges and rightful dignity], so as to assume the guise of a servant (slave), in that He became like men and was born a human being."

PHILIPPIANS 2:9

The Original Text

διὸ καὶ ὁ Θεὸς αὐτὸν ὑπερύψωσε καὶ ἐχαρίσατο αὐτῷ ὄνομα τὸ ὑπὲρ πᾶν ὄνομα.

The NKJV

Therefore God also has highly exalted Him and given Him the name which is above every name.

The NWT

For this very reason, God exalted him to a superior position and kindly gave him the name that is above every other name

Again the word "other" is not in the text. It is not a secondary addition but it is deliberately added to harmonize scripture – their corrupt edition – with the Watch Tower's teachings.

Again, in past editions of the NWT the word "other" stood between brackets. At least the readers knew. Today, a word which is not in the original, a word that changes the meaning of a sentence found in the word of God, is added shamelessly.

"*I am bearing witness to everyone who hears the words of the prophecy of this scroll: If anyone makes an addition to these things, God will add to him the plagues that are written in this scroll; and if anyone takes anything away from the words of the scroll of this prophecy, God will take his portion away from the trees of life and out of the holy city, things that are written about in this scroll.*" (Revelation 22:18-19)

I understand the embarrassment of a body who made its goal to witness to Jehovah and then reads here that Jesus has been given the name – not a name, but the name! – above every name.

It is the Word that has to model our thinking. We must set our minds free from wrong ideas and change according to the revelation found in the Word of God. We are for no reasons authorized to adjust, change or manipulate whatever Bible passage which does not comply with our thoughts or ideas.

TITUS 2:13 – 2 PETER 1:1

Titus 2:13

The Original Text
προσδεχόμενοι τὴν μακαρίαν ἐλπίδα καὶ ἐπιφάνειαν τῆς δόξης τοῦ μεγάλου Θεοῦ καὶ σωτῆρος ἡμῶν Ἰησοῦ Χριστοῦ.

The NKJV
... looking for the blessed hope and glorious appearing of our great God and Savior Jesus Christ.

The NWT
... while we wait for the happy hope and glorious manifestation of the great God and **of our** Savior, Jesus Christ.

2 Peter 1:1

The Original Text

υμεὼν Πέτρος, δοῦλος καὶ ἀπόστολος Ἰησοῦ Χριστοῦ, τοῖς ἰσότιμον ἡμῖν λαχοῦσι πίστιν ἐν δικαιοσύνῃ τοῦ Θεοῦ ἡμῶν καὶ σωτῆρος Ἰησοῦ Χριστοῦ

The NKJV

Simon Peter, a bondservant and apostle of Jesus Christ, to those who have obtained like precious faith with us by the righteousness of our God and Savior Jesus Christ.

The NWT

Simon Peter, a slave and an apostle of Jesus Christ, to those who have acquired a faith as precious as ours through the righteousness of our God and the Savior Jesus Christ.

The little addition of the NWT (*of our*) in Titus 2:13 changes the meaning of the sentence and the deity of Jesus simply disappears from the text.

Such an addition is arbitrary, not required by the context or the Greek grammar. It is simply adopted to harmonize the text with JW's doctrines: since Jesus is not God, the Bible cannot say it must be their reasoning.

My friends, the attitude should be quite the opposite: if the Bible says it, then we must believe it!

Where in the Bible does it say that we are waiting for the glorious manifestation of God and of Jesus? We are waiting for the return of Jesus, he is the subject of this sentence, not God the Father.

A Manual Grammar of the Greek New Testament by H.E. Dana and Julius R. Mantey explains: "When the copulative καὶ connects two nouns of the same case, if the article ὁ or any of its cases precedes the first of the said nouns or participles, and is not repeated before the second noun or participle; i.e., it denotes a farther description of the first-named person."

τοῦ Κυρίου (ἡμῶν) καὶ σωτῆρος 'Ιησοῦ Χριστοῦ.
Of our Lord and Savior Jesus Christ.
2 Pt. 2:20.

The article here indicates that Jesus is both Lord and Savior. So in 2 Pt. 1:1 τοῦ Θεοῦ ἡμῶν καὶ σωτῆρος 'Ιησοῦ Χριστοῦ means that Jesus is our God and Savior. After the same manner Tit. 2:13, τοῦ μεγάλου Θεοῦ καὶ σωτῆρος ἡμῶν 'Ιησοῦ Χριστοῦ, asserts that Jesus is the great God and Savior." p. 147.

As far as 2 Peter 2:20 is concerned, the NWT is correct: "*by an accurate knowledge of the Lord and Savior Jesus Christ.*" But, since 2 Peter 1:1 translated correctly would declare Jesus' Deity, it has been "adjusted" in the NWT to comply with the JW's teachings: "*through the righteousness of our God and* the *Savior Jesus Christ*" while it must read: "*through the righteousness of our God and Savior Jesus Christ,*" since the article "the" is not found in the original text before Savior and the cited grammar rule must be applied here.

We are not looking at opinions or possible – even legitimate – interpretations of Scripture. The Watch Tower openly manipulates the English version of the Bible!

The verses we just quoted tell us that Jesus is God. And if the Word of God says it we are only called to believe it.

Some more devastating evidence concerning the correct translation of 2 Peter 1:1 is found in the NWT itself.

2 Peter 1:1

τοῦ	**Θεοῦ**	**ἡμῶν**	**καὶ**	**Σωτῆρος**	**Ἰησοῦ**	**Χριστοῦ**
of	God	our	and	Savior	Jesus	Christ

NWT: "of our **God and <u>the</u> Savior Jesus Christ"**

I confirm: the JW are not translating another Greek text, they are arbitrarily adding "the" before "Savior" to remove the attribute of "God" for him.

Let us compare **A**. 2 Peter 1:1 with **B**. 2 Peter 3:18. I believe this will prove our case beyond any shadow of a doubt.

A

τοῦ	**Θεοῦ**	**ἡμῶν**	**καὶ**	**Σωτῆρος**	**Ἰησοῦ**	**Χριστοῦ**
of	God	our	and	Savior	Jesus	Christ

B

τοῦ	**Κυρίου**	**ἡμῶν**	**καὶ**	**Σωτῆρος**	**Ἰησοῦ**	**Χριστοῦ**
of	Lord	our	and	Savior	Jesus	Christ

The Greek construction of the phrase is IDENTICAL. Why does the NWT add “the” in 2 Peter 1:1, yet translates 2 Peter 3:18 correctly, as it is in the Greek text, without adding “the”?

“No, but go on growing in the undeserved kindness and knowledge **of our Lord and Savior Jesus Christ**. To him be the glory both now and to the day of eternity. Amen.”

In 2 Peter 1:1 the NWT does not translate the Greek text as it is, but corrupts it to accommodate it to the Watch Tower’s teachings.

The Original Text
7 καὶ πρὸς μὲν τοὺς ἀγγέλους λέγει· ὁ ποιῶν τοὺς
ἀγγέλους αὐτοῦ πνεύματα, καὶ τοὺς λειτουργοὺς αὐτοῦ
πυρὸς φλόγα· 8 πρὸς δὲ τὸν υἱόν· ὁ θρόνος σου, ὁ Θεός, εἰς
τὸν αἰῶνα τοῦ αἰῶνος· ῥάβδος εὐθύτητος ἡ ῥάβδος τῆς
βασιλείας σου. 9 ἠγάπησας δικαιοσύνην καὶ ἐμίσησας
ἀνομίαν· διὰ τοῦτο ἔχρισέ σε, ὁ Θεός, ὁ Θεός σου ἔλαιον
ἀγαλλιάσεως παρὰ τοὺς μετόχους σου· 10 καί· σὺ κατ᾽
ἀρχάς, Κύριε, τὴν γῆν ἐθεμελίωσας, καὶ ἔργα τῶν χειρῶν
σού εἰσιν οἱ οὐρανοί· 11 αὐτοὶ ἀπολοῦνται, σὺ δὲ διαμένεις·
καὶ πάντες ὡς ἱμάτιον παλαιωθήσονται, 12 καὶ ὡσεὶ
περιβόλαιον ἑλίξεις αὐτούς, καὶ ἀλλαγήσονται· σὺ δὲ ὁ
αὐτὸς εἶ καὶ τὰ ἔτη σου οὐκ ἐκλείψουσι.

The NKJV
7 And of the angels He says:
"Who makes His angels spirits
And His ministers a flame of fire."
8 But to the Son He says:
"Your throne, O God, is forever and ever;
A scepter of righteousness is the scepter of Your kingdom.
9 You have loved righteousness and hated lawlessness;
Therefore God, Your God, has anointed You
With the oil of gladness more than Your companions."

10 And: “You, Lord, in the beginning laid the foundation
of the earth, And the heavens are the work of Your hands.
11 They will perish, but You remain;
And they will all grow old like a garment;
12 Like a cloak You will fold them up,
And they will be changed.
But You are the same,
And Your years will not fail.”

The NWT
7 Also, he says about the angels: “He makes his angels
spirits, and his ministers a flame of fire.”
8 But about the
Son, he says: “God is your throne forever and ever, and the
scepter of your Kingdom is the scepter of uprightness.
9 You loved righteousness, and you hated lawlessness. That
is why God, your God, anointed you with the oil of
exultation more than your companions.”
10 And: “At the
beginning, O Lord, you laid the foundations of the earth,
and the heavens are the works of your hands.
11 They will
perish, but you will remain; and just like a garment, they
will all wear out,
12 and you will wrap them up just as a
cloak, as a garment, and they will be changed. But you are
the same, and your years will never come to an end.”

Let us examine this passage in detail.

Verse 8 reads in the original: "πρὸς δὲ τὸν υἱὸν· ὁ θρόνος σου, ὁ Θεός, εἰς τὸν αἰῶνα τοῦ αἰῶνος·"

A faithful, literal translation of this passage must be: "But to the Son He says: "Your throne, O God, is forever and ever."

Since this clearly states that Jesus is God, the NWT found a way to twist it: "But about the Son, he says: "God is your throne forever and ever," which basically tells us that God is the throne of the Son. And I wonder: does it mean anything at all?

This passage is a quotation of a Psalm. Let's see what it says.

In order to be consistent with the New Testament mis-translation of the text, the NWT has "God is your throne forever and ever." in Psalm 45:6 as well. Read the whole Psalm and see for yourself if it makes any sense with this phrase.

The Jewish Virtual Library is a very good website. Their translation of Psalm 45:6 is the following: "Thy throne, O God, is for ever and ever: the sceptre of thy kingdom is a right sceptre"[3]

The 1917 Jewish Publication Society Tanakh reads: "Thy throne given of God is for ever and ever; A sceptre of equity is the sceptre of thy kingdom."

The simple truth is that Hebrews 1:6 calls Jesus God. Too difficult to believe? Well, if this is the case with you, then it only means that you have a problem believing the whole Bible. But, with God and His Word, we cannot play "pick and choose."

---

[3] https://www.jewishvirtuallibrary.org/tehillim-psalms-chapter-45 (05/10/2019)

Some people, I noticed over the years, have what I call a "Thomas attitude." Well, I think that the honest person has been given enough legitimate evidence to start believing in the Deity of our Lord and Savior and like that apostle say:

"Then He said to Thomas, Reach your finger here and behold My hands; and reach your hand here and thrust it into My side; and do not be unbelieving, but believing. And Thomas answered and said to Him, My Lord and my God! Jesus said to him, Thomas, because you have seen Me you have believed. Blessed are they who have not seen and have believed." (John 20:27-29 - MKJV)

Let us continue to consider Hebrews 1.

In verse 10 we find a reference to creation. "At the beginning, O Lord, you laid the foundations of the earth, and the heavens are the works of your hands..."

This passage also is a quotation from the Old Testament, Psalm 102.

If we read it all, we cannot fail to see that the subject of this hymn is Jehovah God and, by consequence, the author of Hebrews is referring to Jesus words that in the Old Testament were spoken of Jehovah and of God!

Read for yourself in the NWT.

> "I said: "O my God, Do not do away with me in the middle of my life, You whose years span all generations.
> Long ago you laid the foundations of the earth, And the heavens are the work of your hands. They will perish, but you will remain; Just like a garment they will all wear out. Just like clothing you will replace

them, and they will pass away. But you are the same,
and your years will never end."
(Psalm 102:24-27 - NWT)

It is there in the Word. It is clear, well said, unquestionably revealed. Now, it's up to the reader to choose whom to believe.

The author of Hebrews speaks of Jesus as God. To him he attributes eternity. Of Him he says:

"He is the reflection of God's glory
and the exact representation of his very being,
and he sustains all things by the word of his power."
(Hebrews 1:3 - NWT)

Can we read of such glory and believe that Jesus is not God? Even if the translation here cannot entirely render the powerful Greek expressions that speak of the Son being the visible manifestation of the invisible, glorious God (John 1:18), at the same time we cannot believe that Jesus can "sustain all things by the word of his power" and still be considered a lesser god, or a creature – this is the prerogative of an Almighty Creator!

May the Lord give us understanding of His Word and faith to believe it.

PART TWO

Textual Problems

INTRODUCTION

In this second part of the book we will evaluate the original text adopted by the Watch Tower for the New Testament and will consider the consequences of this choice on the translation of some of the passages that deal with Jesus' Deity.

I understand that Textual Criticism is not a subject known to the average Bible reader, but discussing the matter, I am sure, will prove to be useful and will give more light to the reader on the reasons why some translations differ from others.

Biblical Textual Criticism is a branch of theological studies which deals with the collation and evaluation of ancient manuscripts of the Bible, in order to give shape to a critical text as close to the lost biblical autographs as possible.

The necessity of textual criticism for the New Testament text arises from the following facts:

1. The autographs are not available anymore.
2. Ancient manuscripts do not have a uniform witness to the text, though not drastically, yet they do differ from one another in some details.

The differences are for less than ten percent of the text and only in few cases the meaning or doctrinal points are altered.

Textual problems are common to all books that were written before the invention of mobile type printing in the XVI century.

In ancient time, manuscript copying was an art and a profession. But, for one reason or another, it was inevitable that the copying process would let some mistakes enter the text. So it is amazing that the New Testament has such an incredible amount of manuscripts witnessing to it with so little variations of the text.

Up until the XIX century, the critical edition of the original Greek New Testament commonly accepted was the so called *Textus Receptus*, TR, or Received Text. It was the one translated by epoch-making Bible versions like the Authorized King James Version of 1611, the Italian and French Bible translated by Giovanni Diodati, or the German Bible of Luther.

In 1881 Westcott and Hort published their edition of the Greek New Testament based on manuscripts that differed significantly form the TR. These two scholars revived the so called Alexandrian/Egyptian text presenting it to the public after the centuries of silence and oblivion to which the Church had relegated it.

All the critics agreed that the TR needed to be reviewed, but not all were satisfied with the results of the revival of the Alexandrian text. This is how the Majority Text party rose. It was formed by those scholars who were convinced that the wonderful, unanimous witness of the vast majority of Greek New Testament manuscripts (over 90 percent of them) was the result of the normal copying process of the autographs and evidence of the preservation of the original text of the New Testament and that the manuscripts diverging from the Majority's witnesses –

which disagree often even among themselves – were only a deviation from the faithful copies of the text.

Today, we basically have three main categories of texts for the New Testament with their relative supporters.

1. The *Textus Receptus*
2. The Alexandrian/Egyptian text
3. The Majority Text

The TR can be viewed as a good text, since it incorporates the Majority Text, yet it has some deviations from it that cannot be defended on grounds of a serious evaluation of manuscript evidence.

The Alexandrian text, which is the most popular today and is championed by the Nestle-Aland and UBS critical texts, reflects the opinion of liberal scholars, who deal with the Bible just like any other ancient book, not considering its inspiration or preservation. In short, today's scholars, who so closely resemble the Alexandrian intellectual atmosphere, are obviously attracted by a text created under circumstances they are comfortable with.

The Majority Text supporters – I am one of them – basically believe that the same text that God inspired, God preserved and that evidence of this is quite visible in the harmony and uniform witness of the vast majority of New Testament ancient manuscripts and of the fathers of the Church.

Where is the great contradiction?

Well, fundamentalists like the JWs or even some Evangelical movements, decide to adopt translations of the Bible which are based on a critical, original text created through principles they would altogether reject.

If the reader is interested in further knowing about this very interesting topic, he or she can read my book on the "Majority Text."

The critical edition I will quote in this section of the book is the famous Zane C. Hodges and Arthur L. Farstad's *The Greek New Testament According to the Majority Text*, Thomas Nelson, 1994. It was published also as a very useful interlinear.

The Majority Text
Θεὸν οὐδεὶς ἑώρακε πώποτε· ‘Ο μονογενὴς Υἱὸς ὁ ὢν εἰς τὸν κόλπον τοῦ πατρός, ἐκεῖνος ἐξηγήσατο.

Westcott and Hort and the Nestle-Aland instead of ‘Ο μονογενὴς Υἱὸς read, μονογενὴς θεὸς

The NKJV
No one has seen God at any time. The only begotten Son, who is in the bosom of the Father, He has declared Him.

The NWT
No man has seen God at any time; the only-begotten god who is at the Father’s side is the one who has explained Him

It is quite a mystery why the champions of the indefinite article add here "the" before "μονογενὴς θεὸς" which they should consistently have translated "an only-begotten god", following the rules they maximized only eighteen verses before this.

Anyway, let us deal with the textual problem.

In ancient biblical manuscripts it was easy to change or mistake the word "Son" for "God" since they were shortened (they are called *Nomina Sacra*) using the first and the last letter of the word. So we had "υἱὸς", "Son", which was abbreviated as "υς", and "θεὸς", "God", abbreviated as "θς."

Honestly, it looks more like a deliberate change than an accidental one.

Probably some Alexandrian scribe aimed at complying with the gnostic heresies which were quite rampant during the first centuries of Christianity right in the Egyptian area.

Let us evaluate the manuscript evidence.

• "Only begotten" reading is supported by a single Latin manuscript.

• "Only begotten God" with no article, P^{66}, Sinaitic, Vatican, C, L.

• "The only begotten God" with the article P^{75}, the minuscle 33.

• "the only begotten Son" the rest of the manuscript evidence!!!

How can few witnesses, contradicting even each other, determine what is the original text of a reading. The very fact that they do not agree among themselves is clear evidence that they are the result of the work of some scribes who evidently overestimated their critical abilities and changed the text according to what they thought it was best – this was a common practice in Alexandria, not relegated to the sacred text, but used also for other ancient books in the famous library there, where – can this be a coincidence? – textual criticism first originated.

The NWT writes “god” with no capital letter. Some versions following the NA/USB text use a capital letter and write “God.” Some even use this passage in support of the Deity of Jesus. I believe that, no matter how you write it, if you add or not an article, the Alexandrian reading has no meaning – if not maybe gnostic.

The Majority Text reading has overwhelming evidence in its favor. If we can ignore 95 witnesses and choose 5, even contradicting each other, the problem is not the evidence we have, but how we deal with it.

The Majority Text
καὶ οὐδεὶς ἀναβέβηκεν εἰς τὸν οὐρανὸν
εἰ μὴ ὁ ἐκ τοῦ οὐρανοῦ καταβάς,
ὁ Υἱὸς τοῦ ‘Ανθρώπου ὁ ὢν· ἐν τῷ οὐρανῷ.

The NA/USB text omit:
ὁ ὢν ἐν τῷ οὐρανῷ

The NKJV
No one has ascended to heaven
but He who came down from heaven,
that is, the Son of Man who is in heaven

The NWT
Moreover, no man has ascended into heaven
but the one who descended from heaven
the Son of man.

The long version of the verse is a very important Christological reference. The logic behind this arbitrary removal from some ancient manuscripts is behind the principles held dear by secular textual critics.

The words are omitted by Vatican, Sinaitic, L, 33, P^{66}, P^{75}.

The rest of the manuscript evidence is against the omission!

The passage is in perfect harmony with the Scriptures. "*Jesus approached and spoke to them, saying: "All authority has been given me in heaven and on the earth.*" (Matthew 28:18 - NWT)

Those who omitted the verse probably had a problem with Jesus being in two places at the same time. But earlier in this same gospel he said: "*Na·than'a·el said to him: "How do you know me?" Jesus answered him: "Before Philip called you, while you were under the fig tree, I saw you.*"" (John 1:48 - NWT)

The Majority Text

Θεὸς ἐφανερώθη ἐν σαρκί, ἐδικαιώθη ἐν Πνεύματι, ὤφθη ἀγγέλοις, ἐκηρύχθη ἐν ἔθνεσιν, ἐπιστεύθη ἐν κόσμῳ, ἀνελήφθη ἐν δόξῃ."

NA/USB read ος instead of Θεὸς.

The NKJV

And without controversy great is the [a]mystery of godliness:

God was manifested in the flesh,
Justified in the Spirit,
Seen by angels,
Preached among the Gentiles,
Believed on in the world,
Received up in glory

The NWT

Indeed, the sacred secret of this godly devotion is admittedly great: 'He was made manifest in flesh, was declared righteous in spirit, appeared to angels, was preached about among nations, was believed upon in the world, was received up in glory.'

This is another change which involves the so called *Nomina Sacra*. The change again, as is seen above, is only of one letter.

Dr. Pickering informs his readers that three-hundred manuscripts have the reading "God" and only seven an alternative.

The truth of the incarnation cannot be shaken by seven witnesses. It is as if we believe the soldiers at the tomb and not the report of the apostles!

With or without the "God" at the beginning of the sentence, the truth revealed here echoes the one that we find in John: "*So the Word became flesh and resided among us, and we had a view of his glory, a glory such as belongs to an only-begotten son from a father; and he was full of divine favor and truth.*" (John 1:14 - NWT)

There is a very important detail, that somehow seems to go unnoticed.

"Oς" at the beginning of the sentence is usually translated "He who was...", or "He was...", but the Greek does not say that and it is simply impossible to be translated, since "ος" at the beginning of a sentence is not "he." Just to give you an idea, it would be as if I talk to you and say: "who told me that he could not do the job." Something is missing! You would look at me with a huge question mark on your face.

They say that Paul's words might be what is left of a Christological hymn, and this would explain the abrupt start. Might be. The fact remains that, if we prefer to abide on evidence and not on suppositions, the only thing to do is to receive the unanimous witness of 99.9% percent of manuscripts, give it up and receive that: "*God was manifested in the flesh...*"

1 JOHN 5:7-8

The long version of the *Textus Receptus*

ὅτι τρεῖς εἰσιν οἱ μαρτυροῦντες ἐν τῷ οὐρανῷ, ὁ Πατήρ, ὁ Λόγος καὶ τὸ Ἅγιον Πνεῦμα, καὶ οὗτοι οἱ τρεῖς ἕν εἰσι· καὶ τρεῖς εἰσιν οἱ μαρτυροῦντες ἐν τῇ γῇ, τὸ Πνεῦμα καὶ τὸ ὕδωρ καὶ τὸ αἷμα καὶ οἱ τρεῖς εἰς τὸ ἕν εἰσιν.

The Majority Text and the NA/USB is basically the same.

ὅτι τρεῖς εἰσιν οἱ μαρτυροῦντες: τὸ Πνεῦμα καὶ τὸ ὕδωρ καὶ τὸ αἷμα καὶ οἱ τρεῖς εἰς τὸ ἕν εἰσιν.

The NKJV

For there are three that bear witness in heaven: the Father, the Word, and the Holy Spirit; and these three are one. And there are three that bear witness on earth: the Spirit, the water, and the blood; and these three agree as one.

The NIV

For there are three that testify: 8 the Spirit, the water and the blood; and the three are in agreement.

The NWT

For there are three witness bearers: the spirit and the water and the blood; and the three are in agreement.

I believe it is fair to say something about this passage of Scripture. I understand many believe in the authenticity of the so called *Johannine Comma*, but it has little if any manuscript support. It is not in the Majority Text. It is not in the Alexandrian text.

The first editions of the *Textus Receptus* did not have it. It was pressure on Erasmus by the people who used the Latin Vulgate that had it that convinced him to add it to his Greek text. From that moment on it became part of it.

The doctrine of the Trinity does not depend on this passage. On the contrary, I am not even sure that the long reading is, theologically speaking, one-hundred percent accurate.

In any case, resting upon evidence, the short text is the original.

PART THREE

The Deity of Jesus in the New World Translation

INTRODUCTION

Not all the Bible passages speaking of the deity of Jesus have been removed from the NWT. In some places it has been impossible for the Watch Tower to remove the witness of Scripture concerning our Lord and Savior's divine nature.

Let us consider these passages.

[26]*Well, eight days later his disciples were again indoors, and Thomas was with them. Jesus came, although the doors were locked, and he stood in their midst and said: "May you have peace."* [27]*Next he said to Thomas: "Put your finger here, and see my hands, and take your hand and stick it into my side, and stop doubting but believe."* [28]*In answer Thomas said to him: "My Lord and my God!"* [29]*Jesus said to him: "Because you have seen me, have you believed? Happy are those who have not seen and yet believe.* (John 20:26-28 - NWT)

How much have we been manipulated and influenced by the Watch Tower not to see the truth so clearly revealed by this passage?

Jesus appears to the apostles and shows that he knows about Thomas' unbelief. How is it possible? Well, he is God. He simply keeps his promise: "*I am with you all the days until the conclusion of the system of things.*" (Matthew 28:20 - NWT)

Thomas was surprised by Jesus words and also he had to acknowledge his actual resurrection.

And in answer to Jesus' invitation to physically realize his resurrection he reacts…

saying

to him

my Lord and my God

John is wrapping up here what he began to say in verse 1 of his Gospel. Jesus is indeed our God! The NWT says it here unquestionably, too! God has not let the witness of the Scripture to be totally removed from the eyes of Jehovah's Witnesses! It's up to the reader to rely on the Word of God for what it says or on the cheap rhetorical false interpretations of the Watch Tower.

1 JOHN 5:20

But we know that the Son of God has come, and he has given us insight so that we may gain the knowledge of the one who is true. And we are in union with the one who is true, by means of his Son Jesus Christ. This is the true God and life everlasting.

"This" of the last sentence of the verse corresponds to the Greek "οῦτός." It must be connected to the last subject and in this case, it is clearly Jesus Christ.

In their interpretation of the passage, jw.org quotes John 17:3 that reads: "This means everlasting life, their taking in knowledge of you, *the only true God*, and of the one whom you sent forth, Jesus Christ." We are called here to believe in the Father and in the Son. Wow! Yes, the Father is *the only true God*. The doctrine of the Trinity does not deny the Unity of God, but it acknowledges also the Deity of the Son of God and of the Holy Spirit, which is revealed in the Scriptures.

We cannot deny certain Scriptural facts because they are simply too complicated to be understood – God Himself, His eternity and power, is beyond human comprehension.

The question is: does the Bible say that Jesus is God? If it does, we are called to believe it.

This passage here reveals that Jesus is God and Life everlasting.

In the same epistle we read:

"*yes, the life was made manifest, and we have seen and are bearing witness and reporting to you the everlasting life that was with the Father and was made manifest to us.*" (1 John 1:2 - NWT). It speaks about Jesus here!

"*And this is the witness, that God gave us everlasting life, and this life is in his Son.*" (1 John 5:11 - NWT)

"*I write you these things so that you may know that you have life everlasting, you who put your faith in the name of the Son of God.*" (1 John 5:13 - NWT)

1 John 5:20 must be understood for what it says. It completes the previous statements in the same epistle who point to the fact that in Jesus was life everlasting revealed.

Jesus boldly said in the gospel of John: "*I am the Resurrection and the Life.*" (John 11:25)

Again he proclaims: "*I am the Way, the Truth and the Life.*"

So after John has called Jesus "God" (John 1:1 and John 20:28) and "Life," here the apostle makes this statement expecting that his readers should not apply his words to Jesus, as they would do by simply reading the text for what it says?

Let's put it this way.

A trinitarian would have used John's language. It is perfectly consistent with the idea that Jesus is God and Life.

But…Would a Jehovah's witness use such an ambiguous language?

He would have paid the utmost attention not to be misunderstood concerning his idea that Jesus is not God.

A Jehovah's Witness could have never written John 1:1, 20:28, 1 John 5:20!

In fact, John was not a Jehovah's Witness, but a witness of Jesus. Jehovah is not found in his epistle, not even one time – see the New World Translation!

Truth is, some passages of Scriptures do not need to be interpreted, but believed. And 1 John 5:20 is among them.

PART FOUR

The Name of God and the New Testament

INTRODUCTION

A very peculiar choice of the NWT is the inclusion of the Name of God, *Jehovah*, in the New Testament.

In 1901 the American Standard Version systematically introduced *Jehovah* in all of the Old Testament Tetragram occurrences. But the use of *Jehovah* also in the New Testament is peculiar of the NWT.

Am I for or against the inclusion of the Divine Name in the New Testament?

This is not the right question and this cannot be the way we approach this topic.

The question is: Was the Old Testament Name of God present in the autographs of the New Testament?

Then, when this question is answered using all the knowledge and the evidence we have, we are entitled to draw our conclusions and abide with them.

The Bible says that the Divine Name was revealed to Moses by God Himself.

In Exodus 3:13-15 we read: "*And Moses said to God, Behold, when I come to the sons of Israel, and shall say to them, The God of your fathers has sent me to you, and they shall say to me, What is His name? What shall I say to them? And God said to Moses, I AM THAT I AM. And He said, So you shall say to the sons of Israel, I AM has sent me to you. And God said to Moses again, You shall say this to the sons of Israel, Jehovah* (יהוה) *the God of your fathers, the God of Abraham, the God of Isaac, and the God of Jacob, has sent me to you. This is My name forever, and this is My title from generation to generation.*"[4]

יהוה is the way the name revealed to Moses is written in Hebrew. (Please notice that Hebrew reads from right to left.)

The Tetragram (from the Greek "Tetragrammaton", which means "four letters") corresponds in our alphabet - more or less - to the following letters: "YHWH."

The Tetragram is translated "Jehovah" in four passages of the King James Version (Exodus 6:3, Psalms 83:18, Isaiah 12:2, 26:4). As we said "The American Standard Version" used *Jehovah* in the Old Testament and so does the Modern King James Version - that's why I am quoting from it here.

Discussing the opportunity to render יהוה as *Jehovah* or *Yahweh*, or in any of the other suggested ways, is not my goal here. Neither it is to investigate the meaning of the Name or Names of God. It is my purpose to ascertain whether the Divine Name was part of the autographs of the New Testament or not and, by logical consequence, if a translator can rightfully restore it in the New Testament or not.

In general, the need of identifying God's Name and restore it has been felt by many translators when dealing with the Old Testament. But what about the New Testament? Are there any grounds to extend such practice to the New Testament?

---

[4] This and the quotations that follow are from the Modern King James Version free on the e-sword Bible software.

There is nothing wrong in studying the Hebrew roots of our Christian faith. I agree that the New Testament itself motivates the inclusion of Hebrew words in our Christian terminology. Words we even use daily like Hallelujah, Amen, Messiah, etc., are clear evidence of such tendency. But the New Testament was originally written in Greek, not in Hebrew, and many Hebrew concepts have been adapted and expressed in the Greek language in which the inspired authors were writing - showing us that there is nothing wrong with translating God's Word. So if someone is trying to force the presence of God's Name (whether they transliterate it *Jehovah* or in any other way), along with those who try to "restore" as much as possible of Hebrew terminology and names in general, we can't help but be skeptical about it.

In fact, not only there isn't enough evidence to believe that the Name was in the autographs of the Greek Scriptures – LXX included – but, on the contrary, there is good evidence that the Divine Name, יהוה, in any of its forms or abbreviations, was not in the original Greek New Testament.

This I will try to discuss shortly in the pages that follow.

MANUSCRIPT EVIDENCE

We have almost six thousand manuscripts of the Greek original of the New Testament, attesting its text, antiquity and reliability. There is no trace in them of יהוה, or of any kind of transliteration of the Name in any way. In all of the Greek New Testament manuscripts, in all the occurrences of the Old Testament passages quoted, where יהוה is found in the original Old Testament Hebrew, we invariably find "*Kyrios*" in the New, which is the Greek for "Lord."

Such was the practice of the Septuagint, the LXX, which is a translation of the Old Testament in Greek as old as the third century BC. Since the New Testament writers wrote in that language, they must have simply and logically followed the LXX practice. Again, unanimous manuscript evidence points in that direction.

I believe this objective fact alone would suffice to end the matter here.

Those who believe that the יהוה was in the autographs of the New Testament and that some kind of conspiracy removed it all together from all the existing copies, have absolutely no evidence to support their views. In doing so, in their blind need to further their fantastic theories, they fail to see that, by accusing ALL manuscript evidence to have been altered so well as to leave no trace at all of such a deliberate falsification, they are undermining the reliability of the text of the very Bible they say they cherish and honor as God's Word.

If we can believe that someone was able to remove or change anything from the Bible and leave no trace at all of such a corruption of the text, then we must also be ready to give up believing the New Testament text as we know it to be reliable.

We thank God that such a possibility is not remote, but unquestionably and scientifically impossible and we can safely trust the text of the New Testament, which has been handed down to us through the centuries, virtually identical to that of the autographs.

To this we must add that not only Greek manuscript show no trace of God's Name in the New Testament, but also all the Christian writers of the first centuries that quote the New Testament know nothing of the presence of the Tetragram in the Greek text. This happens both with the orthodox and the heretic writers - who agree on this. It must be admitted that joined witness of enemies is very reliable.

INTERNAL EVIDENCE

The New Testament text clearly shows that even if its writers had written their books in Hebrew, they would have avoided the use of the Tetragram – which was the common practice of the first century Jewish writers.

Though Jehovah's Witnesses keep on believing that our goal should be to bear witness to the mosaic Name of God, in whatever way we write it or pronounce it, biblical and historical facts point to an entirely different direction.

Jesus himself said: "*But you shall receive power, the Holy Spirit coming upon you. And you shall be* ***witnesses to Me*** *both in Jerusalem and in all Judea, and in Samaria, and to the end of the earth.*" (Acts 1:8)

Christian are Jesus' witnesses! The Bible clearly says so.

Let us consider some statistics concerning the occurrences of the יהוה and of the word God in the Old Testament.

	יהוה	God
The Pentateuch	1934	810
Isaiah	500	138
Jeremiah	736	127
Ezekiel	445	253

As we can easily see, Old Testament authors gave great relevance to the Tetragram. It was the Name that God revealed just before the exodus of the people of Israel from Egypt. In that occasion God gave Moses the Law and He made a covenant with the nation of Israel. יהוה was Israel's Covenant Name of God.

In the New Testament things change. That a change occurred in the relationship of God with man and also with his people, who had rejected the Messiah, is clearly and openly stated by John in his Gospel: "*For the Law came through Moses, but grace and truth came through Jesus Christ.*" (John 1:17)

The New Testament is not Jehovah-centered, like the Old, but Christ-centered.

"*Furthermore, there is no salvation in anyone else, for there is no other name under heaven that has been given among men by which we must get saved.*" (Acts 4:12 - NWT)

Even using Jehovah's witnesses' data, which is clearly an overestimation of the possible presence of the name *Jehovah* in the New Testament, evidence is clear: *Jehovah* is found 237 times, "God" 1363 times.

The tendency of the Old Testament writers has been reversed and the use of the word "God" is overwhelming compared to the places where the JW inserted *Jehovah.* Also, it is worth notice that of the 237 occurrences over 133 are quotations or references to Old Testament passages. This reduces the potential use of *Jehovah* to around 100 occurrences. Less than one tenth of the times the New Testament authors used the word "God."

If the New Testament intended to be "Jehovah witnessing" it is indeed a very poor witnessing.

But if the words of Jesus are to be relied and we have to be *his witnesses* in the preaching of the Gospel, it is natural that this must be reflected in the New Testament words.

Let's see some more statistics.

This is the occurrence of Divine Names in in the New Testament

God	1363
Jesus	1112
Christ	536
Messiah	3
Lord*	680
Father	368
Jehovah*	237
Son of God	236
Savior	24

Even believing the ideas of the JWs are correct, looking at the New World Translation we have 237 references to Jehovah, while the **reference to the person of Jesus** (1112+536+3+236+24) is found about **1911 times**, to which the many times he is called "Lord" should be added.

Can there be any more devastating evidence to the Christ-centered New Testament doctrine?

Also, internal evidence shows that, being their focus on Christ, the New Testament writers had no reason to use the Tetragram when the consolidated practice of the Greek translation of the Old Testament (the Septuagint, in some instances even directly quoted) was to use the word "*Kyrios*", which is "Lord", for every occurrence of the Divine Name.

Why use "Lord"?

Because even as far as the third century BC, it was a consolidated orthodox Jewish practice, as a sign of respect, not to pronounce God's name even when reading the Hebrew Bible.

The Jews encountering the word יהוה in their Bible, even today, read "Adonai", which means "Lord." Hence the Greek translation. Hence the New Testament practice. Hence every reliable translation renders "Kyrios" as "Lord", not corrupting the text, not following opinions and ideas, but simply translating the text of the New Testament as it can be retraced through the manuscript evidence in our possession.

Even through the Greek language reverence for the Name is visible. In fact, New Testament writers show the same attitude of orthodox Jews of the first century in avoiding even the implicit use of God's Name, as statistics data confirms.

Though the whole New Testament was written in Greek, there is a Hebrew version of Matthew that circulated in the Jewish circles and was used in the fourteenth century to dispute Christian doctrine. I believe the way the Divine Name is dealt with in the Hebrew Matthew is very instructive. In every place where Matthew quotes from the Old Testament as well as where the Name is part of significant expressions (like "Angel of the Lord", which in Hebrew includes the Tetragram), the Hebrew text has ה, a short form of "hashem", which means "the Name" – a very common way of reading and addressing the Tetragram among the Jews, even today.

In the rest of the Hebrew Matthew, the Name is avoided, not used! This is quite significant. It tells us that the author of this Gospel showed very deep respect for the Divine Name, and that it is more evident since we are looking at a Hebrew version of a New Testament book.

This same attitude the reader will find in the Hebrew translations of the New Testament, where the Tetragram is obviously retained in the places where the text quotes the Old Testament passages that have it, but not elsewhere in the text.

Internal evidence shows also that in many passages the context in which the apostles write show that they used the word "Lord" and not the Tetragram.

Let's look at just one example.

"[9]*For if you publicly declare with your mouth that Jesus is Lord, and exercise faith in your heart that God raised him up from the dead, you will be saved.* [10]*For with the heart one exercises faith for righteousness, but with the mouth one makes public declaration for salvation.* [11]*For the scripture says: "No one who rests his faith on him will be disappointed."* [12] *For there is no distinction between Jew and Greek. There is the same Lord over all, who is rich toward all those calling on him.* [13]*For "**everyone who calls on the name of Jehovah** will be saved."* [14]*However, how will they call on him if they have not put faith in him? How, in turn, will they put faith in him about whom they have not heard? How, in turn, will they hear without someone to preach?* [15]*How, in turn, will they preach unless they have been sent out? Just as it is written: "How beautiful are the feet of those who declare good news of good things!"* (Romans 10:9-15 – NWT)

Paul wrote in Greek to Christians residing in Rome. If you read carefully his words either you realize that he must have used "Kyrios", "Lord", and not "Jehovah" or you must admit that he is openly identifying Jesus with *Jehovah.*

See the devastating parallel in 1 Corinthians 1:2: "*Paul, called to be an apostle of Christ Jesus by God's will, and Sos'the·nes our brother,* [2] *to the congregation of God that is in Corinth, to you who have been sanctified in union with Christ Jesus, called to be holy ones, together with all those everywhere* ***who are calling on the name of our Lord Jesus Christ**, **their Lord and ours**:...*"

Can we have been so deeply brain-washed not to see something so clearly evident?

THE TETRAGRAM AND THE LXX

Some believe that the ancient manuscripts of the Septuagint can be a key to solving the problem concerning the presence or absence of the Name in the Greek New Testament.

The Papyrus named P. Fouad 266 or also known as Rahlfs 848 is as old as the second century BC. It has the Tetragram in the Hebrew square alphabet, the one we know and which I also used in this article, which is still in use in Israel today. Other ancient Greek manuscripts of the LXX were found with the Name in paleo-Hebrew script, the alphabet in use before the square script alphabet came into use. The singularity of the scribal behavior has led someone to conjecture that the Septuagint, though a Greek translation, originally retained the Divine Name in Hebrew letters.

Professor George Howard, whose merits are undisputed, but whose conclusions I strongly oppose, set forth a theory: "that the divine name, יהוה (and possibly abbreviations of it), was originally written in the NT quotations of and allusions to the OT and that in the course of time it was replaced mainly with the surrogate" Greek word we translate in English as "Lord". (see *Journal of Biblical Literature, The Tetragram and the New Testament*, 96/I (1977), 63-83).

I fail to see the reasons for the Jehovah's Witnesses' excitement concerning Howard's theories. They quote him as if he was giving any sanction to their practice of using Jehovah in the New Testament. On the contrary, he clearly states that: the New Testament originals might have had the original Hebrew words for the Tetragram (יהוה) or its common Hebrew abbreviation (ה) – not Jehovah! – but only when quoting from the Old Testament. Also, the fact that some ancient LXX manuscripts had the Name in Hebrew, is openly contrary to the use of Jehovah, that for a Jew might be as good as any other surrogate - since Jehovah is neither the transliteration of the Hebrew into our alphabet nor the way it is read. Jehovah's witnesses are used to quote authorities that, when fairly considered, are against their views. Professor Howard has been writing to the Watch Tower for a long time to lament this misuse of his work, but without any result.

Albert Pietersma has written a very deep and valuable article on this subject: "Kyrios or Tetragram: a renewed quest for the original LXX." There he gives convincing evidence that the presence of the Tetragram in some LXX manuscripts is due to the need of harmonization with the Hebrew text felt by some scribes or religious groups. Specifically, in dealing with the witness of the above mentioned P. Fouad 266 or Rahlfs 848, he writes: "it contains at least half a dozen instances of correction to the Hebrew text. Some revising of this text has obviously been done in order to bring it in better accord with the Hebrew." Pietersma concludes: "In the Pentateuch kyrios (which means "Lord") as a surrogate for the tetragram is original."

In this perspective the testimony of the LXX to the Name assumed by Howard in order to develop his theory must be reconsidered altogether. His idea of the presence of the Tetragram or of the abbreviation of it, is not substantiated and cannot be considered anything more than a theory at best. In fact, evidence points to another direction than that suggested by Howard: the presence in some manuscripts of the original Hebrew name of God in a Greek translation must be seen as a trace of deliberate attempts of Jewish scribes to improve the text of the Septuagint, bringing it to a more evident dependence from the Hebrew original. It can be no matter of discussion the fact that the scribe inserting יהוה at the place of kyrios would not expect the fruiters of his work to read יהוה in any other way than "*Adonai*", which is equivalent to "*Kyrios*" in Greek and "Lord" in English.

The Septuagint testimony is in favor of the use of "*Kyrios*", "Lord", by New Testament authors also where they quote from Old Testament passages. They simply followed in the footsteps of the Septuagint, using "*Kyrios*."

CONCLUSIONS

As I said earlier, no evidence is so strong against the inclusion of יהוה in the New Testament like the witness of all the existing Greek manuscripts.

In the days of the early Church, there were only local, independent groups (churches) connected one to another by bonds of love, but no central authority existed which could impose whatever idea, practice or text to all of Christianity. It is self-evident that the New Testament books must have circulated for some time independently. They must have been used and copied by heretics also and, in general, by different emerging factions in Christianity.

It is practically impossible that something that occurred in all or almost all the books of the New Testament could be obliterated from manuscript evidence without leaving any trace at all in any of the surviving manuscripts. Not with the incredible amount of evidence we have of the original Greek text.

Avoiding to argue about the possible renderings of the Tetragram, I conclude that the serious, honest translator of the New Testament - in order to remain such and not become an editor of the text - must abide with the witness of the New Testament and translate "Lord" every occurrence of "*Kyrios.*"

Of course the Hebrew translations of the New Testament must be an exception, since they should diligently render the Old Testament quotations including the Name. Of course the Tetragram will be read by Jews "*Adonai*", which means "Lord" and corresponds to the Greek "Kyrios" – which is the reading adopted by the New Testament.

For all the above facts, the only possible conclusion of this discussion is that, as far as evidence is concerned, no translator has the right to discard the apostolic choice to include "Lord" (Kyrios in the original Greek) in the New Testament text, even in the quotation of Old Testament passages that, in the original Hebrew, included the Divine Name. All attempts to "restore" the Name, in any of its suggested readings, are not to be encouraged or supported, since they do not improve the text, nor translate it, but represent a corruption of the text of the New Testament as preserved in all the ancient manuscript evidence.

PART FIVE

Conclusion

CONCLUSION

It is time to draw our conclusions on the accuracy and reliability of the text of the New World Translation.

It is very sad to see how evident it is the discrepancy between the words used on the JWs' official website and the poor state of the text, the total lack of accuracy and even of good faith that emerges when one sees evidence for what this Bible "translation" is really about.

On www.jw.org they write boldly, with a convincing and charming language, in order to seduce the unaware, the unsuspecting people who meet them on their way before having been alerted by those who either left the organization or have enough biblical knowledge to understand that the things taught by the Watch Tower are a misrepresentation of the Christian doctrine and that their Bible has been conceived only to substantiate or motivate some of their unscriptural beliefs.

During the past forty years I have known many people, even friends, that have fallen prey of the diabolical ways of persuasion used by the Jehovah's Witnesses to further not God's kingdom but the growth of the Watch Tower organization.

I do not like to argue with them. Most of the times I did it was just a waste of time. They are either too brainwashed to listen, or know nothing of the original languages, they just repeat the lesson they know by memory and are not able to judge the accuracy of what you try to explain to them. Very cunningly the organization builds walls and barriers before sending the witnesses out so that any attempt to talk to them, to convince them of anything contrary to the Watch Tower, is simply frustrating and practically useless.

I felt the need to write this book in order to equip Christians against JWs' lies on the original text of the New Testament and its translation. I also hope that some "witness" may be more easily reached by a book than by personal contact.

I wrote this book out of love not for the desire of contention. So my prayer goes out to all the honest and sincere believers among the Jehovah's Witnesses, that they may seek Jesus and be set free from the bondage of religion and sectarianism of which they are a victim.

If the Son sets you free,
you will be truly free.

John 8:36 – NWT

APPENDIX A

Journal Of Biblical Literature: Philip Harner: Qualitative Anarthrous Predicate Nouns

(Edited by Joseph A. Fitzmyer, 1973, Vol 92 p. 85)

In light of this examination of John's usage we may turn to the verse in which we are especially interested, 1:1. Our study so far suggests that the anarthrous predicate in this verse has primarily a qualitative significance and that it would be definite only if there is some specific indication of definiteness in the meaning or context. As an aid in understanding the verse it will be helpful to ask what John might have written as well as what he did write. In terms of the types of word-order and vocabulary available to him, it would appear that John could have written any of the following:

A. ho logos en ho theos

B. theos en ho logos [what John actually wrote]

C. ho logos theos en

D. ho logos en theos

E. ho logos en theios [see footnote 24]

Footnote 24: ["The word *theios* appears only a few times in the NT: Acts 17:27 (v. 1.), 29; Tit 1:9 (v. 1); 2 Pet 1:3, 4. It is not used in the Fourth Gospel. But presumably John could have used it, or some other word meaning "divine," if he had wished to do so.]

Clause A, with an anarthrous predicate, would mean that logos and *theos* are equivalent and interchangeable. There would be no *ho theos* which is not also *ho* logos. But this equation of the two would contradict the preceding clause of 1: 1, in which John writes that ho logos *'nv theos.* This clause suggests relationship, and thus some form of "personal" differentiation, between the two. Clause D, with the verb preceding an anarthrous predicate, would probably mean that the logos was "a god" or a divine being of some kind, belonging to the general category of *theos* but as a distinct being from *ho theos.* Clause E would be an attenuated form of D. It would mean that the logos was "divine," without specifying further in what way or to what extent it was divine. It could also imply that the logos, being only *theios,* was subordinate to *theos.*

John evidently wished to say something about the logos that was other than A and more than D and E. Clauses B and C, with an anarthrous predicate preceding the verb, are primarily qualitative in meaning. They indicate that the logos has the nature of *theos.* There is no basis for regarding the predicate *theos* as definite. This would make B and C equivalent to A, and like A they would then contradict the preceding clause of 1:1.

As John has just spoken in terms of relationship and differentiation between *ho* logos and *ho theos,* he would implying B or C that they share the same nature as belonging to the reality *theos.* Clauses B and C are identical in meaning but differ slightly in emphasis. C would mean that the logos (rather than something else) had the nature of *theos.* B means that the logos has the nature of *theos* (rather than something else). In this clause, the form that John actually uses, the word *theos is* placed at the beginning for emphasis.

Commentators on the Fourth Gospel, as far as I know, have not specifically approached the meaning of this clause from the standpoint of the qualitative force of *theos* as an anarthrous predicate preceding the verb. In many cases their interpretations agree with the explanation that is given above. But consideration of the qualitative meaning of *theos* would lend further clarification and support to their understanding of the clause. J. H. Bernard, for example, points out that Codex L reads *ho theos* instead of *theos.* 'But this," he continues, "would identify the Logos with the totality of divine existence, and would contradict the preceding clause. [J. H. Bernard, A *Critical and Exegetical Commentary on the Gospel according to St. John* (New York: Scribner, 1929) 1, 2.] In a similar way W. F. Howard writes that *theos* and *ho* logos are not interchangeable. Otherwise, he continues, "the writer could not say 'the Word was with God.' [W. F. Howard,

The *Gospel according to St. John* (IB 8; New York: Abingdon-Cokesbury. 1952) 464.] Both writers, in effect, are arguing that the predicate *theos* cannot be regarded as definite in this clause. In terms of our analysis above this would mean that clause B should not be assimilated to clause A.

Bruce Vawter explains the meaning of the clause succinctly and lucidly: "The Word is divine, but he is not all of divinity, for he has already been distinguished from another divine Person. [B. Vawter, *The Gospel according to John* (JBC; Englewood Cliffs, N. J.: Prentice Hall, 1968) 422.] But in terms of our analysis it is important that we understand the phrase "the Word is divine" as an attempt to represent the meaning of clause B rather than D or E. Undoubtedly Vawter means that the Word is "divine" in the same sense that *ho theos* is divine. But the English language is not as versatile at this point as Greek, and we can avoid misunderstanding the English phrase only if we are aware of the particular force of the Greek expression that it represents.

In his discussion of this clause R. E. Brown regards the translation "the Word was God" as correct "for a modern Christian reader whose trinitarian background has accustomed him to thinking of 'God' as a larger concept than 'God the Father.' [R. E. Brown, *The Gospel according to John,* I-XII (AB 29; Garden City: Doubleday, 1966) 5.]

Yet he also finds it significant that *theos* is anarthrous. Later he adds, "In vs. Ic the johannine hymn is bordering on the usage of 'God' for the Son, but by omitting the article it avoids any suggestion of personal identification of the Word with the Father. And for Gentile readers the line also avoids any suggestion that the Word was a second God in any Hellenistic sense. [Brown, *John, I-XII, 24.]* In terms of our analysis above, Brown is arguing in effect that clause B should be differentiated from A, on the one hand, and D and E on the other . [Brown *(John, I-XII, 25)* also mentions the view of De Ausejo that throughout the prologue the term "Word" means Jesus Christ, the Word-become-flesh. "If this is so," he comments, "then perhaps there is justification for seeing in the use of the anarthrous *theos* something more humble than the use of *ho theos* for the Father." But if *theos is* qualitative in force, it is not contrasted directly with *ho theos.* John evidently wished to say that the logos was no less than *theos,* just as *ho theos* (by implication) had the nature of *theos.]*

Rudolf Bultmann's explanation of the clause also reflects an appreciation of the qualitative force of *theos* without specifically recognizing it as such. The clause means first, he suggests, that the Logos is equated *(gleicbgesetzt)* with God; *"er war Gott."* [R. Bultmann, *Dai Evangelium der Johannes* (Meyer *2;* G6ttingen: Vandenhoeck & Ruprecht, 1968) 16.] Bultmann means by iliis that we must not think in terms of two divine beings, in a polytheistic or gnostic sense. [Bultmann, *Johannes,* 16-17.] Thus he guards against assimilating clause B to D or E. But he explains further that this equation between the two is not a simple identification *(einfache Identifikation),* because the Logos was *pros ton theon.* [Bultmann, *Johannes, 17.]* In this way he guards against assimilating B to clause A. Bultmann's interpretive instinct at this point is unquestionably sound. In terms of the analysis that we have proposed, a recognition of the qualitative significance of *theos* would remove some ambiguity in his interpretation by differentiating between *theos,* as the nature that the Logos shared with God, and *ho theos* as the "person" to whom the Logos stood in relation. Only when this distinction is clear can we say of the Logos that "he was God."

These examples illustrate the difficulty of translating the clause accurately into English. The RSV and *The Jerusalem Bible* translate, "the Word was God." *The New English Bible* has, "what God was, the Word was." *Good News for Modern Man* has, "he was the same as God." The problem with all of these translations is that they could represent clause A, in our analysis above, as well as B. This does not mean, of course, that the translators were not aware of the issues involved, nor does it necessarily mean that they regarded the anarthrous *theos* as definite because it precedes the verb. But in all of these cases the English reader might not understand exactly what John was trying to express. Perhaps the clause could be translated, "the Word had the same nature as God." This would be one way of representing John's thought, which is, as I understand it, that *ho logos,* no less than *ho theos,* had the nature of *theos.*

At a number of points in this study we have seen that anarthrous predicate nouns preceding the verb may be primarily qualitative in force yet may also have some connotation of definiteness. The categories of qualitativeness and definiteness, that is, are not mutually- exclusive, and frequently it is a delicate exegetical issue for the interpreter to decide which emphasis a Greek writer had in mind. As Colwell called attention to the possibility that such nouns may be definite, the present study has focused on their qualitative force. In Mark 15:39 1 would regard the qualitative emphasis as primary, although there may also be some connotation of definiteness. In John 1:11 think that the qualitative force of the predicate is so prominent that the noun cannot be regarded as definite.

In interpreting clauses of this type it is important to recall that Greek writers also had other types of word-order available. If a writer simply wished to represent the subject as one of a class, he could use an anarthrous predicate noun after the verb. If he wished to emphasize that the predicate noun was definite, he could supply the article. The availability of these other types of word-order strengthens the view that in many instances we may look primarily for a qualitative emphasis in anarthrous predicate nouns that precede the verb.

Source: http://www.bible.ca/trinity/trinity-Harner.htm

BIBLIOGRAPHY

Ante-Nicene Fathers, Hendrickson Publishers, Peabody, Massachusetts, USA, 1994

DANA H. E. and MANTEY J. R. – *A Manual Grammar of the Greek New Testament*. Prentice Hall, 1955.

HARNER, P. – *Qualitative Anarthrous Predicate Nouns* in Journal Of Biblical Literature, Edited by Joseph A. Fitzmyer, 1973, Vol 92 p. 85

HODGES, Z. C. and FARSTAD A. L. – *The Greek New Testament According to the Majority Text*, Thomas Nelson, 1994

LIGHTFOOT J. B. – *St. Paul's Epistles to the Colossians and Philemon*. Hendrickson Publishers. 1875. 1995.

MACHEN J. G. – *New Testament Greek for Beginners*. The Macmillan Company. 1923.

MOUNCE W. D. – *A Graded Reader of Biblical Greek*. Zondervan Publishing House. 1995.

WALLACE D. B. – *Greek Grammar Beyond the basics*. Zondervan. 1995.

YOUNG R. A. – *Intermediate New Testament Greek, A Linguistic and Exegetical Approach.* Broadman and Holman Publishers. 1994.

ABOUT THE AUTHOR

Giuseppe Guarino was born in Catania, Italy, 1968.

He is author of several books, many of which deal with the original languages of the Bible, such as his New Testament Greek manual, written both in his native tongue, Italian, and in English.

Updates on his books and articles will be found on his personal website: www.giuseppeguarino.com

Printed in Dunstable, United Kingdom

76446874R00078